BARTOLVS.
A.
SAXO FERRATO.

BARTOLUS

ON THE

CONFLICT OF LAWS

TRANSLATED INTO ENGLISH

BY

JOSEPH HENRY BEALE

ROYALL PROFESSOR OF LAW
IN HARVARD UNIVERSITY

THE LAWBOOK EXCHANGE, LTD.
Clark, New Jersey

ISBN 978-1-58477-294-1

Lawbook Exchange edition 2003, 2025

The quality of this reprint is equivalent to the quality of the original work.

THE LAWBOOK EXCHANGE, LTD.
33 Terminal Avenue
Clark, New Jersey 07066-1321

*Please see our website for a selection of our other publications
and fine facsimile reprints of classic works of legal history:*
www.lawbookexchange.com

Library of Congress Cataloging-in-Publication Data

Bartolo, of Sassoferrato, 1313-1357.
 Bartolus on the conflict of laws / translated into English by Joseph
Henry Beale.
      p. cm.
 Originally published: Cambridge [Mass.]: Harvard University Press,
1914.
 Includes bibliographical references.
 ISBN 1-58477-294-8 (cloth: alk paper)
    1. Conflict of laws—Early works to 1800. I. Title: Conflict of laws. II.
Beale, Joseph Henry, 1861-1943. III. Title.

K7040 .B364 2003
340.9—dc21   2002038864

Printed in the United States of America on acid-free paper

BARTOLUS

ON THE

CONFLICT OF LAWS

TRANSLATED INTO ENGLISH

BY

JOSEPH HENRY BEALE

ROYALL PROFESSOR OF LAW
IN HARVARD UNIVERSITY

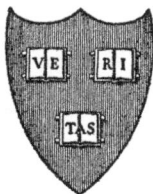

CAMBRIDGE

HARVARD UNIVERSITY PRESS

LONDON: HUMPHREY MILFORD
OXFORD UNIVERSITY PRESS

1914

THE UNIVERSITY PRESS, CAMBRIDGE, U.S.A.

TO THE

UNIVERSITY OF PERUGIA

WHERE THE SEED OF LEGAL KNOWLEDGE WAS
SOWN IN THE MIND OF BARTOLUS, AND
BROUGHT FORTH FRUIT AN
HUNDRED-FOLD

BARTOLUS

ON THE

CONFLICT OF LAWS

BARTOLUS

ON THE CONFLICT OF LAWS

INTRODUCTION

BARTOLUS of Sassoferrato is the most imposing figure among the lawyers of the middle ages. To him, in particular, is ascribed the first and standard statement of the doctrines of the Conflict of Laws. For although his predecessors had thought and written on the subject, and his own work professes to be based throughout on previous authority, his text is the starting point and the cited authority for all subsequent work on the subject for five hundred years. "The reign of Bartolus was long at the bar and in legal science. Some called him the father of law, others the lamp of law. They

[9]

said that the substance of truth was found in his works and that advocates and judges could do no better than to follow his opinions." [1]

In the course of five hundred years the simple principles which Bartolus laid down became strangely warped and distorted. The various schools of statutists in Italy, France, and the Netherlands drew singular conclusions from his expressed opinions and ascribed these conclusions too often to Bartolus himself.[2] Through Dumoulin, Voet, and Huber these new conclusions became the basis of much modern speculation, through the work of Story, Mancini, and Foelix.

These facts must be the excuse for publishing, on the six hundredth anniversary of his birth, a translation of his treatise on the Conflict of Laws. The translator can

[1] 1 Laurent, Droit Civil International, 299.
[2] 1 Lainé, Introduction au droit international privé, 131.

urge as a qualification neither an adequate command of the Latin language, knowledge of medieval law, nor English style; but those better qualified have unfortunately neglected the work. The translation has purposely been made freely, with the hope of making the work in that way clearer to American lawyers. Those references which deal with questions of the Conflict of Laws have been extended and translated, since only thus can the work of Bartolus himself be separated from that of his predecessors. Extracts from a short "Life of Bartolus," by Savigny, follow.[1]

Bartolus was born in Sassoferrato, a town in the Duchy of Urbino, in 1314. His family name, Severi, was after his death changed to Alfani. At the age of fourteen years he began to study law at Perugia, under Cinus, and continued there several years; he afterwards studied at

---

[1] Geschichte des römischen Rechts, vi. 137–184.

Bologna, under the celebrated professors Buttrigarius, Rainerius, Oldradus, and Belvisio, and received the doctor's degree in 1334. The succeeding five years were passed in study, and he then became an assistant judge at Todi and at Pisa. He began to teach at Pisa in 1339 and at Perugia in 1343, and his great reputation began with his teaching at Perugia. His most famous pupils were Baldus and Angelus de Ubaldis, both born in Perugia. He became free of the city of Perugia, at the petition of the university, in 1348. In 1355 he was ambassador at the court of the Emperor Charles IV, then at Pisa, and received many favors from the Emperor. He died at Perugia in July, 1357, in his forty-fourth year, and was buried in the church of St. Francis; on his tomb is found the simple but all-sufficient epitaph: *Ossa Bartoli*. The fame of Bartolus, continues Savigny, surpasses that of every jurist of the middle ages; a fact all the more remarkable because he died at an age when many celebrated jurists are just beginning to be known.

Bartolus was married to the Lady Pellina Bovarelli and left at his death two sons, Franciscus and Aloysius, and four daughters, Sancta, Paula, Francisca, and Nella. His will, which is preserved, shows the returns for scholarship in the middle ages to have been ample. To charity and to relatives outside his family he left one hundred thirty-five pounds and one hundred florins in gold. To each of his daughters he gave a dowry of four hundred fifty florins in gold. To his wife and daughters he left in money, beyond their dowries, two hundred twenty florins. The residue he left to his two sons.

Nearly three hundred years after his birth (in the year 1590) he had living numerous descendants in the eighth and ninth generations. In the male line in the eighth generation a biographer enumerates nineteen males.

His work on the Conflict of Laws comprises a portion of his Commentary on the Code (Super Primam et Secundam Partem Codicis Commentaria). This was printed often and early. Hain notes an undated edition, without imprint (2539); Riessinger, 1471 (2540); Vindelimus, 1471 (2541); Gerretzem, Venice, 1476 (2542; British Museum 500 k. 1); Jenson, Venice, 1478 (2543; B. M. 5205 c. B. M. has also the Jenson edition with 1477 imprint, 5205 i. 4); Mantheu, Venice-Cologne, 1480 (2544); Mauser, Venice, 1482 (2545); Pachel, Milan, 1483 (2554; Bodl. has 1484); Zanis, Venice, 1486 (2552); Toresan, Venice, 1488 (2546); Pachel, Milan, 1490 (2547; B. M. 5306 h); Anon., Naples, 1491 (2548); Catarensis, Venice, 1490 (2553); Toresan, Venice, 1492 (2549;

B. M. 5205 h); de Tortis, Venice, 1493 (2550); de Tortis, Venice, 1499 (2551).

In the sixteenth century notices have been found of the following editions: Lyons, 1518, 1521, 1549, 1550, 1563; Venice, 1570; Turin, 1574; Basle, 1592. A collected edition of Bartolus' works was published in Venice, 1588, 1590, 1602–3, 1615. The sections upon the Conflict of Laws were reprinted in the Appendix to Guthrie's "Savigny's Conflict of Laws," 2d ed., 1880; from which edition, corrected in a few instances from the edition of 1602, the present translation has been made.

BARTOLUS, COMMENTARY UPON JUSTINIAN'S CODE

DE SUMMA TRINITATI
gloss *QUOD SI BONONIENSIS*[1]

I

NOW let us come to the gloss which says "if a Bolognian makes a contract at Modena, he shall be judged by the statute of Modena." As to this, two things are to be noticed: first, whether a statute extends beyond its territory to those not subject; second, whether the effect of a statute extends beyond the territory of the legislator. And first, I ask, what about contracts? Suppose a contract celebrated by a foreigner in this city: a contest arises, and suit is brought in the place where the contract was made: of what

[1] Code I. 4, gloss.

place should the statutes be observed or looked at? Since these questions are much discussed, let us omit other distinctions, and examine the questions more fully than the doctors have done. We either speak of statute or custom with respect to the form of the contract itself, or the suit on it, or with respect to jurisdiction over the performance provided for in the contract itself.

(§ 14). In the first case the law of the place of contracting governs.[1]

(§ 15). In the second case, the question either concerns matters which pertain to the form of action, and then the law of the forum governs;[2] or it concerns the merits of the litigation itself: either matters which arise out of the contract itself, at the time it is made, or matters which arise *ex post facto*, out of negligence or delay in performance.

---

[1] Dig. xxi. 2. 6; Code 6. 32. 2.
[2] Dig. xxii. 5. 3 *in fin.*

(§ 16). In the former case, the law of the place of contract governs;[1] by which I understand the place where the contract is made, not the place of performance; for though a sale of land is to be carried out where the land is, yet the law of the place of making the contract of sale governs. And this is the opinion of Dinus.[2]

(§ 17). This doctrine does not apply in the case of dowry, for a reason stated in the text.[3]

(§ 18). In the case where the dispute arises out of negligence or delay in performance, either performance is fixed in a certain place: or several places in the alternative, so that there is an election for the performance; or in no place, because the promise was made without condition. On

[1] Dig. xxi. 2. 6.

[2] [Dinus († 1298), professor of law at Bologna, teacher of Cinus, who in turn was teacher of Bartolus. The passage referred to is his commentary on Dig. xliv. 7. 21.]

[3] Dig. v. 1. 65.

the first supposition, the custom in the place in which the performance is fixed governs; on the second and third suppositions, the place where payment is sought governs, because the negligence or delay happened at that place.[1]

(§ 19). By what has been said many questions may be solved. There is a statute at Assisi, where a contract of dowry and marriage is celebrated, that if the wife dies without children, the man shall enjoy the third part of the dowry. But in this city of Perugia, from which the husband comes, there is a statute that the husband shall enjoy half. Which governs? Certainly the statute of the husband's domicile.[2] Another example: there is a statute here that the right of suing for a debt is prescribed in ten years. Now a Florentine borrowed one hundred in the

---

[1] Dig. xii. 1. 22; xiii. 3. 4; and especially xxii. 1. 1 *in prin.*, with the gloss to the word *contractum.*
[2] Dig. v. 1. 65.

Roman court under contract to return it in the city of Perugia. Certainly if he did nothing for ten years the statute here will apply because the negligence was a violation of our statute; but this seems contra to the gloss,[1] where it seems to be said that not the place of the contract but of the judgment governs. Certainly that gloss is wrong.

(§ 20). But here William[2] solves the problem in this way. We are either speaking of where the contract treats of matters of common concern according to the contract of the defendant and by provision of the contracting parties, and then the place of the contract governs;[3] but in those things which come unexpectedly, as when they happen in connection with the perform-

---

[1] Dig. xiii. 4. 2.
[2] [William of Cuneo († 1348), professor of law at Toulouse and at Orléans, author of Commentaries on the Digest and the Code.]
[3] Dig. xxi. 2. 6.

ance of the contract, then the place of the judgment governs.[1] So he says, but his words have not the savor of truth. For the rule of law is that the custom of the place where the contract is made governs.[2]

Let me say briefly this: either one wishes to seek restitution for a breach happening in the contract itself at the time of contracting, when we look to the place of contracting, or from a breach happening after the contracting from other circumstances such as delay, and we look at the place where the delay happened, as appears from the foregoing. And so if it were in the place of the judgment we look at the place of the judgment, and in that case that gloss may tell the truth, otherwise it is false.

[1] Dig. xlvi. 3. 98.
[2] Dig. l. 17. 34.

II

SECOND, I ask what about delicts. If a foreigner does a wrong here shall he be punished according to the statutes of this city? This question is touched by Cinus.[1] Let us put it broadly: either what he did in this city is wrong by the common law; then he is punished according to the statutes or custom of this city,[2] as Dinus and James of Arena[3] and all say: or it was not a wrong by the common law, and then either the foreigner

---

[1] [Cinus de Pistoia (1270–1336), professor of law at Trevisa, Siena, Perugia, and Florence; teacher of Bartolus, Dante, and Petrarch; author of Lectures on the Digest and on the Code.] See also Code 8. 53 (52). 1.

[2] Code 3. 15 and Auth.; Dig. xlvii. 11. 9; Decretal 5. 39. 21 and gloss. Code 3. 24. 1 is not opposed to this; see the annotations of Cinus.

[3] [Jacobus de Arena, professor of law at Padua, Naples, Reggio, and Siena; author of Lecturae or Additiones to the gloss.]

had lived so long in the city that he really ought to know the statute, and then it is the same case;[1] or he had not lived there long, and then the act was either commonly prohibited by all cities (as, for instance, that he should not carry grain outside the territory without license from the government, which is commonly prohibited throughout all Italy) and in that case he should not allege ignorance as a total excuse:[2] or it is not so generally prohibited, and then he is not held unless he knew of it.[3] And there is now a text for this,[4] where an ignorant man is not held unless his ignorance was gross and supine.

---

[1] Code 3. 15. 2 and note in the last gloss.
[2] Dig. xxxix. 4. 16. § 5.
[3] Dig. l. 9. 6.
[4] Sext. I. 2. 2 (*ut animarum*) and gloss.

III

THIRDLY, I ask what in the case of a will? Suppose there is a statute or custom at Venice that a will shall be valid before two or three witnesses. A foreigner makes a will there. Is it valid? On this general question first, we must see whether the custom or statute is valid; second, if it is valid whether it applies in the case of a foreigner.

[The discussion of the validity of the custom in §§ 22, 23 is omitted.] (§ 24). As to the second point, whether such a custom extends to a foreigner: James of Arena decided that it did not.[1] Furthermore, he said, though it be granted to the country people that they may make a will before five witnesses, nevertheless this is not allowed to anybody who happens to

---

[1] Code 6. 23. 9; Dig. xlix. 14. 32.

be in the country;[1] and besides, as a statute is called the law proper to a city it does not extend to strangers.[2] But it seems to me we should say either the statute affects the persons of citizens and does not extend to foreigners;[3] or the statute speaks simply and indefinitely, and applies to foreigners there making wills.[4] For as to those things which are of voluntary jurisdiction, a statute binds foreigners.[5] Besides, it is so in contracts,[6] as we have said above; therefore, etc.[7]

---

[1] Dig. xxix. 7. 8.

[2] Dig. i. 1. 9.

[3] So I understand Code 6. 23. 31 in connection with Dig. xxix. 7. 8. § 1.

[4] Code 6. 32. 2.

[5] Code 8. 48. 1; for this I cite in especial Dig. xxix. 1 *ult.*

[6] Dig. xxi. 2. 6.

[7] I say this, notwithstanding Code 6. 23. 9, because I understand it according to the distinction indicated; and Dig. xlix. 14. 32, because it speaks about hostages, who are not Roman citizens and have no capacity to make a will (Dig. xxviii. 1. 11), and it is therefore necessary for them to accept the toga and become citizens, and then make a will

We now come to the question whether such a will extends to goods which are elsewhere, where there is no such custom. But as to this, doubt is raised whether, if the statute disposes with regard to a person (as, what son of a family can make a will); and if a foreign son of a family makes a will in that city, the will is valid. I say no, because statutes cannot legitimate a person not subject to them, nor can they make any disposition about such a person.[1] And this, notwithstanding what has been said above about form. For the form of an act pertains to the jurisdiction of the city in whose territory it is done; so it varies according to the difference in places;[2] but wherever there is a difference of person, a statute cannot dispose, except about a person subject to it.

---

according to the custom of their locality, as above shown.

[1] Dig. xxvi. 5. 1 *in fin.*; xxvi. 1. 10 and note.
[2] Dig. xxii. 5. 3; xxix. 3. 2. § 7.

But the opposite of what has been said is found in the Code,[1] where a person not subject is legitimated according to the form of a statute. I answer, that statute does not legitimate the person directly, because it cannot; but it gives the form and solemnity for creating legitimation there, as for instance that emancipation shall be made there before such a court. When, therefore, it has to do with form, it extends to foreigners. And so I say, if a statute provides for restraining a person, as for instance, a statute says a man cannot make his wife an heir; certainly if a foreigner makes a will here it does not prevent him making his wife an heir for the said reasons. This is held in the *Speculum Juris*.[2]

---

[1] Code 8. 49. 1.

[2] [Gulielmus Durantis (1237–96), professor of law at Modena, wrote the Speculum Juris, a practical treatise on the Roman law, which was so celebrated that he was known as "Speculator." The passage referred to is Speculum Juris (ed. 1602), pt. ii, p. 785; tit. *de sen.*, *qualiter*, ver. *item pone*.]

IV

FOURTH, I ask what about those things which are neither contracts nor delicts nor last wills? Suppose one has a house here, and it is a question whether he can raise it higher. Briefly, when there is a question of any right growing out of a thing itself, the custom or statute of the place where the thing is should be observed.[1]

(§ 28). I ask whether statutes and customs of the laity bind the clergy? [This portion of the text, containing §§ 28–31, is omitted in this translation.]

---

[1] Code 8. 10. 3; Dig. viii. 4. 13. § 1.

V

SIXTH, we must see whether statutes or customs may extend their effect outside the territory; which must be examined by many lines of questions; because some statutes are prohibitive not by reason of a penalty but by reason of some solemnity; some are permissive; some prohibitive. About the first class I say this: such statutes are either prohibitive by reason of the solemnity required for some act, as where the statute says that a will or instrument shall not be made except before two notaries or some other solemnity; then such a statute does not extend beyond the territory of the legislator, because in matters of form we always look to the place where the thing is done, as has been said above both about contracts and about last wills. Or the statute is pro-

hibitive *in rem*, and with respect to a
thing, as where it prohibits the title of
property to be passed between husband
and wife. Then wherever a disposition of
such a thing is made it is not valid, because
such a provision affects the thing and
prevents the title passing.[1] Or the statute
is prohibitive *in personam;* and then it
either contains a favorable prohibition, as
for instance, in order that young persons
shall not be deceived in the making of
wills it is provided that one under fifteen
years old cannot make a will; or suppose
the statute is that a man cannot make
a legacy to his wife, or the opposite, and
this is done lest by reason of their mutual
love they may despoil or deceive one
another; then such a prohibition includes
a citizen of that city wherever he is.
Similarly, it is understood generally in the

---

[1] Inst. 2. 8; Dig. xxii. 5. 1; Code 5. 13. 15;
Code 6. 3. 3; Code 8. 10. 3.

case of one who is interdicted in dealing with his goods. For such an interdiction, which is favorable, so that his goods shall not be wasted, extends its effect wherever the goods are.[1] For the same reason the special interdiction for a particular act is the equivalent of an interdiction general and special.[2] (§ 33). If on the other hand the statute contains a burdensome prohibition, then it does not extend beyond the territory of the legislator.[3] And so I say that a statute providing that a daughter as a woman shall not succeed, since it is prohibitive and burdensome,[4] does not extend to goods situated elsewhere.[5]

---

[1] Dig. xlv. 1. 6; xxvii. 10. 10.
[2] Dig. xlix. 17. 11; xxvi. 7. 51.
[3] Dig. iii. 1. 9.
[4] Code 6. 28. 4.
[5] On this distinction between prohibitions which are rational, favorable, or burdensome see Sext. 5. 11. 26.

VI

SEVENTH, I ask about permissive statutes, about which two things are to be said, first, whether a permissive act may be done outside the territory of the permitting law; and second, if it is exercised in the very way or place which the law permits, whether it takes effect outside the territory? And these two things we treat together; for always a statute allows and permits what it does not reasonably forbid, excepting those things in which a privilege is specially granted; for instance, by the statute of a city one is made a notary; can he execute an instrument outside the territory of that city? About this Speculator treats.[1] My own opinion is that instru-

---

[1] Speculum Juris (ed. 1602), pt. ii, p. 662; tit. *de instr.*, § *restat*, ver. *quid de his.*

ments cannot be made outside the territory; and so of similar things that may be done within the territory. (§ 35). For acts which pertain to voluntary jurisdiction when allowed to an inferior by the prince, cannot be exercised outside the territory.[1] (§ 36). Yet I suppose that instruments executed by such a notary within his territory have force everywhere outside the territory. So an emancipation executed before one who has jurisdiction by the local law has force everywhere;[2] and this is so because it is rather a matter of form than of substance.

Sometimes statutes are permissive in that they allow what is already permitted by the common law, but they remove out of the way some requirement of the common law. And this happens in many ways.

---

[1] Dig. i. 16. 2, which is noteworthy on this point; Sext. 2. 2. 1 *in fin.*

[2] Code 8. 49. 1.

Sometimes a requirement of form is abolished. Suppose seven witnesses are required by law for a will, and the statute provides that four shall be enough; this statute is certainly valid. And if it is a question whether a will made in the territory shall be observed as to the testator's goods outside the territory, this question is treated by several authors, for instance by Hubert of Bobis [1] and other ancient Ultramontanes, whose opinions Speculator cites,[2] but their conclusion is not clear. Afterwards came James of Ravenna,[3] who said that the heir should have the goods within the territory, but the goods which are outside the territory those should

---

[1] [Ubertus de Bobio, professor at Parma in 1227, then at Vercelli and at Modena. One of the later glossators.]

[2] Speculum Juris (ed. 1602), pt. ii, p. 679; tit. *de instr. edit.*, § *compendiose*, ver. *quid si.*

[3] [Jacobus de Ravanis († 1296); by birth a Frenchman, professor at Toulouse, 1274; "the first jurist who applied the forms of dialectic to the science of law." His works are lost.]

have who take upon intestacy.[1] It is no
objection that he would thus die in part
testate and in part intestate,[2] because
difference of custom would cause it, as, in
the case cited, difference of patrimony.[3]
And of the same opinion was Cinus once;
afterwards came William of Cuneo, who
said the will was good without distinction,
and extended to the goods everywhere,
even outside the territory. This he proved,
first, because the statute operates upon
the will itself, and if that was valid from
the beginning, the effect extends from the
will itself to all the goods by consequence;
and though the statute cannot dispose of
the goods directly, yet it may by consequence.[4] Furthermore, as a proper action
may be instituted elsewhere, where the
land lies, so a disposition may be made

[1] Dig. xxvi. 5. 27; xxvi. 7. 47.
[2] Dig. l. 17. 17.
[3] Dig. i. 7. 22.
[4] Dig. xxvi. 4. 3. § 1; Inst. 1. 17.

elsewhere, where the *res* is.[1] Besides, an
act before one judge has force before another.[2] Moreover, in his opinion this very
case is covered by the Code;[3] if a will is
made before a judge, where a minor form
is required, then the inheritance may pass;
and this transfer has effect everywhere.
And of this opinion afterwards was Cinus,
and made an addition in his lecture, though
he did not recite his opinion in full. Doctor
William of Cuneo and Doctor James
Buttrigarius[4] held the same.[5] This opinion pleases me, for the aforesaid reasons,
except the first reason of William, which
displeases me, as I will now explain. For
confirmation of the aforesaid I cite the
Code *de testamentis*,[6] where a will made in

---

[1] Code 7. 33. 12.
[2] Code 2. 1. 2; 7. 62. 15 and 19; 6. 23. 31.
[3] Code 6. 23. 19.
[4] [Jacobus Buttrigarius († 1348), teacher of
Bartolus; author of Lectures on the Digest and the
Code.]
[5] Code 6. 23. 9; 6. 32. 2.　　　[6] Code 6. 23. 31.

the country before five witnesses has its
effect everywhere, although the stricter
form may be required in another place.
Furthermore, a will made in the army takes
effect everywhere, and the custom of the
region is looked to with regard to the form
of any act about which a question is raised,[1]
and so I should hold. But William's first
reason does not please me. What is not
directly permitted is to be sure sometimes permitted by way of consequence;
that is, when that which is not permitted
directly is a *necessary* consequence of the
antecedents, otherwise not.[2] But if the
will is valid, it does not necessarily follow
that it should pass all the goods. Reason:
because by force of law one may die testate
in part and intestate in part, as in the case
of a soldier.[3]

---

[1] Dig. xxv. 4. 1.
[2] Dig. xxxiv. 3. 29; iii. 2. 4. § 2; note by Dinus
to Dig. xxvi. 8. 1.
[3] Dig. xxix. 1. 3 and 41; Code 5. 9. 1 and note.

(§ 38). But sometimes permissive statutes are found which remove a limitation of personal quality. For instance, a statute provides that a minor son (*filius familiae*), or some other person forbidden by law, may make a will; or it is provided in a statute that a bastard may be made heir — things which are forbidden at common law. Suppose, for the present, that such statutes are valid; I will speak of that elsewhere; I shall not now speak of their validity. (§ 39). The question is, whether such a person may be made heir outside the territory, and take up the inheritance. I say no. Since this is the legislation of some power inferior to the sovereign, its force cannot extend beyond the jurisdiction of the legislating power, though it relates to a voluntary act.[1] On this point see the Code and the modifying Novel,[2]

[1] Dig. i. 16. 2.
[2] Code 5. 27. 8; Nov. 89. c. 4.

where the legitimation of a son which is by grant of a city court has no force except between the applicant father and son, not as to the grandfather, nor *inter alios*. So in the case in point, a legitimacy created by the statute of a city has no force except in the legitimating city.

(§ 40). But a strong and constantly recurring doubt rises as follows. One thus legitimated makes a will in that city, or is made heir there, and undertakes the inheritance; is such a will valid, or does the inheritance so undertaken extend to goods which are in another city? And it is said that they do, according to what has been said about statutory provisions as to mere form.

(§ 41). Moreover, to the same effect is the provision of the Code about emancipation,[1] for the emancipation there created has force everywhere; as is said above

---

[1] Code 8. 49. 1.

about the person of a notary. Furthermore, execution will be ordered by a judge in one territory, even upon goods situated there, of the unexecuted judgment of a foreign judge.[1] So this will, which is a *quasi* judgment,[2] extends to goods there placed.[3] Furthermore, "simple disposition" cannot be understood, except of goods which are in the territory of the disposer.[4] For this the expression seems to be the passage in the canon,[5] where it is said that legitimacy created by the Pope does not extend to things which are not of his jurisdiction, as to inheritance and other temporalities, which are in the Emperor's jurisdiction, where note also the gloss of William and modern doctors.

---

[1] Dig. v. 1. 45; Code 3. 1. 13. § 3.

[2] Dig. xxviii. 1. 1.

[3] But see, to the contrary, that it does not extend, Dig. xxvi. 5. 27; xxvii. 1. 10. § 4.

[4] Dig. xlii. 5. 12. § 1; Auth. *quib. mo. nat. effi. sui,* § *filium,* where the legitimation is understood to be strictly made.   [5] Decretal 4. 17. 13.

I answer to the contrary. For a provision about the form of an act is a different thing from the legitimation of a person for an act. Reason: because when there is a difference of place, different reasons exist for different results. For in the case of a military will fewer witnesses are required, since by reason of military occupation so many men cannot be had, and therefore in that case provision is made for a smaller number of witnesses. It may be, too, that in one city there are more legal men than in another, and therefore the statutes are different. That reason of form, therefore, has force outside as well as in the city with respect to the will. So the law has provided that so far as form is concerned its effect is recognized everywhere. For there is no prejudice here to another city, for that act could be done anywhere, though not in that form. But a provision about legitimating a person for doing an act is not of this kind; so I cannot legitimate except in so far as I am myself the disposing power; nor has my act force outside my territory, because it would cause prejudice to another.[1] And this is true, notwithstanding the provisions of the Code about emancipation, and what has been said above about notaries; because there the statute does not directly make provision for an act, but for the form of an act. For the statute does not emancipate the son, for that would empower him abroad, but the father emancipates the son, using the form provided by the statute. So in case of the notary; for he takes no part in the disposition itself, but in solemnizing an act done by another, wherefore there is the same reason so often stated as to form. This is true notwithstanding what has often been said about a judgment; for there the judge disposes about a right

---

[1] Code 8. 49. 1.

already vested and created, a right which follows the person everywhere; therefore execution is allowed by another judge. But when a judge acts *de novo* by creating a right within the territory, then it has no force outside the territory, as has been proved above.

(§ 42). But doubt may be raised on some such question as this. It is the custom of England that the eldest son succeeds to all the goods. Now one having goods in England and in Italy dies; the question is, what law governs. James of Ravenna and William of Cuneo hold that as to goods in England judgment is given according to the custom of that place; while as to those in Italy, they are distributed at common law, and divided between the brothers.[1] Though a certain form is given for goods situated there, it does not extend everywhere.[2] Cinus holds the same here.

[1] Dig. xxvi. 5. 27. [2] Code 10. 1. 4; Dig. l. 1. 24.

Others say that the place where the inheritance vests should be looked to, just as if a contract were made there,[1] since in contracts we look to the place of contracting.[2]

It seems to me that the words of the statute or of the custom are diligently to be examined. For either the provision is made about a *res*, as by these words: The goods of decedents shall go to the first-born, and then I should adjudicate as to all the goods according to the custom or statute at the place where the things are situated; for the law affects the things themselves, whether they are possessed by a citizen or a stranger:[3] or else the words of the statute or of the custom make provision about a person, as by these words: The first-born shall be heir; and then either

---

[1] Dig. xlii. 4. 3.
[2] Dig. xxi. 2. 6.; l. 17. 34.
[3] Dig. l. 4. 6; Code 8. 10. 3.

such decedent was not an Englishman,
though he had possessions there, in which
case such a statute does not affect him and
his sons, because a provision about persons
does not affect foreigners, as was said
above: or such decedent was English;
and then the first-born succeeds to the
goods which are in England, and to the
others he succeeds at common law, according to what the said doctors say;
because either this is said to be a statute
which deprives the younger sons, in which
case, since it is odious, it does not affect
goods situated abroad, as was proved
above, or you call the statute permissive
in removing an obstacle so that the younger
sons may not interfere with the elder,
and that is the same, as has been said
above.[1] (§ 43). Nor am I satisfied with
the opinion of those who look at the law

---

[1] On this point, that one should examine whether
a provision is *in rem* or *in personam*, see Dig. xviii.
1. 81.

of the place of taking up the inheritance; for taking up the inheritance cannot be of importance except on the question of how far the inheritance is delayed.[1] But it is not delayed, except in the way indicated, that is, where no one takes it up, etc. But contracts extend as far as the will of the contracting party goes; which is presumed to have been according to the custom of the place where the thing is done, as has been said above; therefore, etc.

[1] Dig. v. 4. 3.; xxix. 2. 10 and 75.

VII

EIGHTH, about punitory statutes. This is to be investigated along many lines of question. First, whether they may extend their force expressly outside the territory? To which I say, that sometimes either the delinquent or he against whom the crime is committed outside the territory is a foreigner; then the rule is that the statute, though it expressly forbids the act, does not extend to those persons who are outside the territory, etc.,[1] because the statutes are the peculiar right of the city.[2] This rule fails in cities confederated and bound together; as if a statute of Perugia provided that a delinquent at Assisi might be punished here.[3]

---

[1] Dig. ii. 1. 20.
[2] Dig. i. 1. 9.
[3] Dig. xlix. 14. 7 *in fin.*

The same is true, I suppose, for the same reason, if the state in whose territory the crime was committed had consented to the making of the statute.

Sometimes a foreigner offends a citizen beyond the territory of the city, and a statute provides that the foreigner should be punished here; would this be valid? It has been held so, just as a layman offending a clerk is tried in the ecclesiastical court.[1] (§ 45). Moreover, by reason of the place in which a crime is committed, everyone is subject to that jurisdiction, even a stranger.[2] But if the crime is committed in a place subject to the city, upon the person of its citizens, therefore, etc. But those reasons do not cover this case. In the case put of the offense against a clerk, the reason is that he commits sacrilege, which is an ecclesiastical crime, and

---

[1] Code 1. 3. 2; Auth. *item nulla;* Decretal 2. 2. 8.
[2] Dig. i. 18. 3; Code 3. 15. 1 and Auth. *qua in prov.*

therefore pertains to the church. And
that phrase which runs, by reason of the
place, etc., I understand to mean, by reason of an immovable thing, like territory,
not of a movable or self-moving thing.
State the rule thus, therefore; such a statute is not valid, because a city cannot
legislate beyond its territory upon persons
not subject to it.

There is an exception in the case of
thieves from a wreck, who may be punished
by the judge of the person offended; and
so, when such a crime pertains to persons
of its jurisdiction a statute may be made
against such delinquents outside the territory,[1] though the opinion of Cinus is contrary. Another exception is in the case
of federated cities, as I have said before.
Another exception, where my fellow citizen offends and the judge of the place does

---

[1] Dig. xlvii. 9. 7 and gloss; though Cinus would
not hold this in his comment on Auth. *qua in prov.*

not punish the offense (either because he will not, or because he cannot), then a statute against the offending citizen may be made outside the territory.[1]

Sometimes a citizen commits an offense outside the territory; and a statute expressly applies to such an offense committed outside. I suppose such a statute is valid, because by reason of origin he may be punished for a crime committed anywhere;[2] therefore since such an offense is within the jurisdiction, a statute about it may be made.[3]

(§ 46). In addition to the cases considered, this doubt may be raised. Suppose the army of one state is occupying the territory of another and one foreigner kills another there; may he be punished by the

---

[1] Code 1. 9. 14 with gloss, and our master, 23. q. 2c. For this I cite Innocent, Decretal 2. 2. 14, where he expressly holds the statute valid.

[2] Code 3. 15. 1.

[3] Dig. l. 9. 6 and particularly Code 4. 42. 2 and Code 4. 63. 4.

Power of the former state? It seems not, though expressly so provided by statute, as has often been said. Custom observes the contrary rule. It is thus proved. Territory is so called from terrifying.[1] But while the army of this state is there, terrifies and coerces that place, properly an offense there committed may be punished by the sovereign, although committed in that territory; as Nicolas Matarellus and James Buttrigarius held.

(§ 47). Likewise I ask what if it were not expressly provided in the statute, but the statute spoke simply, would it extend beyond the territory? For this investigation I put the question previously examined. It is provided by the statute of the city of Perugia that the Power may inquire of any homicide whatever, or proceed by accusation or by inquisition. It is provided in another statute that a certain

---

[1] Dig. l. 16. 239. § 8.

penalty shall be imposed for homicide. It happens that a Perusian kills outside the territory; the question is whether the Power of this city may inquire and punish according to the form of the statute, or only at common law. This question was put by Odofredus [1] and decided that there can be no proceeding by inquisition, nor can the delinquent be punished according to the form of the statute, but only at common law; whose opinion Albertus of Gandino [2] puts in the end of his book. Afterwards Doctor Cinus disputed the question in the city of Siena, and determined to the contrary, touching on the principles of Odofredus, though no mention of them was made; therefore I recite his disputation here, omitting many unnecessary things:

[1] [Odofredus († 1265), author of **Commentaries** on the Digest and Code.]

[2] [Albertus of Gandino (probably thirteenth century), author of *Quaestiones statutorum.*]

It is certain that at common law a delinquent may be punished at the place of his domicile or origin for an offense committed elsewhere.[1] With this premise let us see whether one may proceed by way of accusation only, that is, at common law, or by way of inquisition by the municipal law. And it seems that it is only by accusation. For at common law inquisition is made for public vengeance[2] and not undertaken for punishing delicts.[3] But the injury seems not to be done except in the place where one committed the delict, not in the place of his origin.[4] Therefore the judge of origin should not proceed or inquire. Besides, the rulers of a state are called the fathers of their subjects,[5] but a foreigner harmed outside the territory

[1] Code 3. 15. 1; Dig. xlviii. 22. 7. §§ 9. 13.
[2] Nov. xvii. 4. 2.
[3] Auth. lxxxvi. c. 3, *de armis*, § *sancimus*.
[4] Dig. ii. 1. 7 and 9.
[5] Auth. lxxxvi. 3, *de armis*, § *sancimus;* Auth. viii. 8, *ut judices*, § *eos antem.*

is not subject to the judge of the offender's country of origin, who therefore is not as a father to him and cannot properly proceed concerning an injury done him. On the other hand, since he may proceed because he has jurisdiction at common law, as has often been said, therefore he may use that jurisdiction with the statutory quality added that he may proceed by inquisition.[1] Besides, this is proved by reason of the city's especial interest. For it is for the interest of the republic to have good subjects.[2] But men are made good by imposing penalties on them for delicts;[3] and that is expressly given as the reason for public discipline for them.[4] Therefore the interest of a Power is to punish its subjects, and so the statute extends to

---

[1] Dig. ix. 4. 4. § 4.
[2] Dig. i. 6. 1. § 2 and Auth. viii, praef. § 1, *ut jud.*, § *cogitatio.*
[3] Dig. i. 1. 1. 1.
[4] Dig. xxxix. 4. 9. § 5.

them. And moreover, for the same reason, it seems that the procedure should be either by accusation or by inquisition; for an inquisition takes effect in place of the accusation.[1] Moreover, suppose Titius beyond the territory violated the Code about Bishops and Clerks,[2] it is certain that the judge by reason of origin may inquire; and so in the case in point. Moreover, the statute speaks generally; therefore, etc.[3] For these reasons Cinus decided that a judge may rightly proceed by inquisition and denunciation, as well as by accusation; and I will presently say whether this is correct.

But about another point, that is, condemnation, it seems first that he should be punished by the law of the place where he offended.[4] Contracts and delicts

[1] Dig. ix. 2. 32.
[2] Code 1. 3. 10.
[3] Dig. xxxvii. 5. § 1.
[4] Code 3. 24. 1.

have been regarded as equivalent,[1] but in contracts the place of the contract is looked at,[2] as has been proved above; therefore, etc. Moreover, it has been said above, near the beginning of this tract, that the place of the delict ought to be looked at: therefore, etc.[3] On the other side, that he may be punished according to the law of his own city, it is proved thus: the law and the judgment are of equal power.[4] But he may bind his subject by his judgment: therefore by his law. Moreover, if anyone commits a crime in a church, which it is evident is not of the secular jurisdiction, nevertheless he may be punished by the secular judge by his law.[5] Besides, this is expressly approved by the Code[6] where the

---

[1] Dig. v. 1. 20 and 57.
[2] Dig. xxi. 2. 6.
[3] Sext. 1. 2. 2, *ut animarum.*
[4] Dig. xl. 1. 9.
[5] Code 9. 9. 1, Auth. *si quis.*
[6] Code 4. 42. 2.

subject is bound even outside the territory.
From which Cinus determined that a citizen may be punished in his own city according to the law of his city. If it is asked how could the effect of a statute extend beyond the territory, he himself answers: I confess that it cannot create a new substantial obligation outside the territory, but it may well add a new quality to that delict which is of common law, which is affected more easily than a new substantial change is made.[1] And this notwithstanding the Canon *ut animarum*, because that decision proceeded from error of the canonists, or is peculiar to the judgment of excommunication. This is the effect of their words.[2]

(§ 48). Now it seems to me the words of the statute should be more diligently

---

[1] Dig. ix. 4. 4. § 3.
[2] The foregoing is taken from the words of Dig. ii. 1. 20.

examined. For it either provides expressly
for that which the citizen does even outside the territory, and then he may be
proceeded against and punished outside
the territory;[1] or it speaks narrowly of
that which is within the territory, and
then it does not extend to those things
which are done outside;[2] or the statute
speaks simply, and that is the question
under discussion, and I shall speak of that
case. Either it is a question of form of
proceeding; then it is possible to proceed
according to the statute of the city where
the suit is instituted, because statutes
with respect to process or the institution
of litigation extend to every suit which is
brought in that city, although the cause
of action is something done outside the
city,[3] as has been said above with regard

[1] Dig. iv. 42. 2.
[2] Dig. xxiv. 3. 64. § 9.
[3] Dig. xxii. 5. 3; xxix. 3. 2 *in fin.;* Code 1. 3. 25
in fin.

to contracts; [1] and so on the first point one must hold the opinion of Cinus, that procedure may be by inquisition: or you are asking about the form of punishment; then he is punished either at common law or according to the statute of the place where he committed the wrong, because statutes which have to do with the substance of the suit do not extend to those things which happened outside the territory, but the place where the thing is situated should be looked to, as has been said above, both about contracts and about delicts, and this is the case in the Canon *ut animarum;* [2] and in this I hold the opinion of Odofredus and Albertus of Gandino. (§ 49). So let the judge be cautious when he forms the inquisition that he say at the end of the inquisition: "upon these things all and singular I

[1] Code 9. 4. 1.
[2] Sext. 1. 2. 2 *ut animarum,* § 1; Dig. xlii. 5. 12. § 1.

intend to proceed and inquire according to the form of the statutes of this city, and to punish the guilty, and condemn according to the form of law." And so in procedure he refers himself to the statute and in condemning to the common law.

VIII

FINALLY I ask about the effect of a judgment for punishment, whether its effect extends beyond the territory of the judge. And omitting all citations I state what I think; distinguishing into different heads, for sometimes punishment is sought with regard to person, sometimes with regard to property. In the first case either the punishment imposed respects interdiction for a certain place, and then it does not extend beyond the territory of the interdict by the power of the judgment, though it does extend to some places by consequence and disposition of law;[1] or it does not respect an interdiction of a certain place, but of a certain kind, and then it does not extend beyond the territory.[2] But when it does

---

[1] Dig. xlviii. 22. 7. §§ 1. 10.   [2] Dig. iii. 1. 9.

not principally respect interdiction of place or of kind, but diminution of status, as when one is rendered infamous, then his status is regarded as diminished, or he is enslaved as a penalty, and then too his status is diminished.[1] And in the first case the penalty imposed here has its effect everywhere;[2] so much more, I say, in the case of those who are enslaved as a penalty by judgment; for in them diminution of status is effected, though solely by way of punishment.[3] If then it is owing to the kind of punishment, I do not care whether such penalty is imposed by the form of a statute or by common law.[4] And according to this I suppose that that mother who was here condemned to fire, and afterwards was received by her

---

[1] Dig. l. 13. 5. §§ 1. 3.
[2] Dig. iii. 1. 9.
[3] Dig. iii. 1. 29; Dig. xlviii. 19. 14; Code 5. 16. 24.
[4] See Dig. iii. 2. 22 and notes.

family, at once became a slave as punishment, even according to the law to-day.[1] For it should not affect the case after judgment: and so wherever she is I say that she is slave by punishment, nor can she make a will or contract or do other such things. And I say the same thing in the case of excommunication, because excommunication is decreed everywhere.[2] For those penalties which respect diminution of status are inflicted upon the person and follow the person as leprosy does the leper.[3]

In the second case, when the punishment is with respect to goods, suppose one is condemned in the city to forfeiture of goods; he has some goods elsewhere: are they forfeited? William of Cuneo touches

---

[1] Dig. xlviii. 19. 29 and notes; Code 5. 16. 24 and Auth. there; but to-day see Nov. xxii. 8.

[2] Decretal 1. 6. 43. q. 5.

[3] Dig. xlviii. 19. 3 *in prin.*, with gloss *fi. p. socio.*

this,[1] and holds that each city should have the goods situated in its territory; for the goods are regarded as *bona vacantia*,[2] and those taking from the intestate are cut out. Therefore when a city has the character of the *fiscus*, the goods so far as they are in the territory fall to it.[3] To this effect is the Code about Bishops and Clerks,[4] where the church has part of the goods, and the court, the *fiscus*, or the patron has part.[5] Others say, as Nicolas Matarellus[6] in his disputation says: either the judge who forfeited the goods has jurisdiction by common law and imposes a penalty according to the process of common law, or

[1] Also Dig. iv. 5. 2.
[2] Code 10. 10. 1.
[3] Dig. vii. 2. 3.
[4] Code 1. 3. 20.
[5] Dig. l. 15. 4. § 2; xxvi. 5. 27; xxvii. 1. 30. § 1. And see Code 10. 19. 10; 10. 10. 2.
[6] [Nicolas Matarellus, professor at Modena, 1279, and later at Padua, abridged the works of Odofredus.]

he has his jurisdiction and power to punish by a municipal law or some such thing. In the first case such a punishment extends to the property wherever situated, but incorporation into the *fiscus* is made by that officer in whose territory the goods are situated;[1] as when there are several guardians of the same infant having his property in different cities or provinces, and one of them in one province is entitled to the possession of the goods which are in another,[2] so here several officers in different provinces represent one *fiscus*. In the second case, when one thing or the other comes from the municipal law, then the forfeiture does not extend to goods which are not subjected to that jurisdiction.[3] It seems to me that one should say on this question that a city cannot

---

[1] Dig. xlii. 1. 15. § 1; xlii. 5. 12. § 1 and note; Code 10. 10. 2 and 5.

[2] Dig. xxvi. 7. 39. § 3.

[3] Code 5. 34. 5.

forfeit goods to itself on account of a delict at common law,[1] and a city at common law does not have mere *imperium* and cognizance of the more serious crimes.[2] Therefore those cities of Italy which exercise that jurisdiction and forfeit goods to themselves do this either by reason of privilege conferred on them by the prince or by ancient custom which has the force of a constituted privilege;[3] and so the cities which now have a fiscal chamber may be called procurators of the *fiscus* for their own interest in the city. For by grant they use the fiscal power for their own interest. (§ 51). With this premise I give my opinion as follows on the preceding question. Either the jurisdictions are separate, but the fiscal purse is one in effect in the two places, or they are separate

---

[1] Code 10. 10. 1.

[2] Code 1. 55. 5.

[3] Dig. xliii. 20. 3. § 4; xxxix. 3. 1 *in fin.;* Auth. xv. 1. §§ 1 *de defens.*

jurisdictions and separate fiscal purses. In the first case that forfeiture may be made at common law, and in that case the goods in both places will be forfeited,[1] and execution shall be made by the officer of the place where the goods are, as has been said above: thus I am of opinion that if the president who represents the Roman church in the Marquisate of Ancona should forfeit the goods of anyone at common law, they should be regarded as forfeited goods which he has in the Duchy, but in those goods execution should be made by the procurator of the *fiscus* who is in the Duchy. On the other hand, forfeiture may be made according to the constitution or special laws. Then on the one hand those special laws may be in force in every place where there are goods: for example, several judges are deputed by a single king for different territories of the kingdom, one

---

[1] Code 10. 10. 2.

forfeits according to the royal constitution, then all goods which are in the kingdom are forfeited for the same reason and by the same laws. On the other hand the said special laws are not common to both places. In the Marquisate there are several constitutions which are not in the Duchy; then such forfeiture does not extend to goods which are outside the place to which the constitution applies.[1]

In the second case, when the jurisdictions are distinct, either the forfeiture is not at common law, and then it does not extend to other property, even elsewhere situated, by the said laws, or it happens at common law, and then it extends to all goods, even situated elsewhere. Nevertheless each shall have the property situated in its own territory, according to what William of Cuneo said, which I approve:

---

[1] Dig. ii. 1. 20; Sext. 1. 2. 2 *ut animarum;* Code 5. 34. 5; Dig. xxvi. 5 *in fin.* and 27.

our city is called the procurator of the *fiscus*, as has been explained above. But if it be a procurator of the *fiscus*, the acceptance and incorporation of the said goods into the *fiscus* pertains to the use of the *fiscus* and to his office, as has been said: therefore now it belongs to the *fiscus* and to its use.[1] Nor should one distinguish whether the judge has jurisdiction, but only this: whether he gives judgment upon that which is permitted to him by common law or in accordance with a new provision of law, as I have said above.

---

[1] To this effect see Dig. xxvi. 8. 22; Decretal 2. 2. 14.

APPENDIX

EXTRACTS FROM THE DIGEST OF JUSTINIAN

i. 1. 1. § 1. We desire to make men good, not only by putting them in fear of penalties, but also by appealing to them through rewards. (Monro's tr.)

i. 1. 9. All nations which are governed by statutes and customs make use partly of law which is peculiar to the respective nations, and partly of such as is common to all mankind. Whatever law any nation has established for itself is peculiar to the particular state (*civitas*), and is called civil law, as being the peculiar law of that state. (Monro's tr.)

i. 18. 3. The *praeses* of the province has a right of *imperium* over the men of his own province only, and he has the right only while he is in the province; if he leaves it he becomes a private person. Sometimes he has *imperium* even over outsiders, if they commit any active offense; it is part of the instructions given by the Emperor that the governor of the province shall take measures for ridding the province of evil-disposed persons, and no distinction is made as to the place from which such persons come. (Monro's tr.)

ii. 1. 20. An officer who exercises jurisdiction outside his local limits may be disobeyed with impunity. The same rule holds where he affects to exercise jurisdiction with reference to an amount beyond his competency. (Monro's tr.)

iii. 1. 9. When a man is forbidden to move on behalf of others on some ground which does not entail infamy, and consequently does not deprive him of the right to move on behalf of others in every case, he is only disabled from moving on behalf of others in the province in which the magistrate who pronounced the prohibition was *praeses;* the prohibition does not extend to any other province, though it should bear the same name. (Monro's tr.)

v. 1. 20. The correct view is that every kind of obligation is to be treated like [one founded on] contract, so that, wherever a man incurs an obligation, it is to be held that a contract was made there, though it should not be a case of a debt founded on a loan. (Monro's tr.)

1. 45. A banker ought to be sued where

the contract with him was made, and no ad-
journment of the case should be allowed save
on sufficient grounds, [for example,] to allow
of his books being brought from a province.
A similar rule holds with reference to an action on guardianship. Where the guardians
of a girl have judgment given against them
in the province in an action which they de-
fended on behalf of their ward, the curators
of the girl are compellable to obey the decree
in Rome, the fact being that the girl's mother
borrowed the money in Rome, and the girl
was her mother's heir. (Monro's tr.)

v. 1. 65. A woman ought to sue for her
dos where her husband's home was, not where
the written assurance of *dos* was made; the
contract of *dos* is not of such a kind that
regard should be had to the place where the
assurance was executed so much as to the
place where the woman herself would have
naturally made her home in consequence of
the marriage. (Monro's tr.)

viii. 4. 13. § 1. If it is understood that
there are stone quarries on your land, no one
can hew stone there . . . unless indeed there
is a custom existing in those quarries to the
effect that, should anyone desire to hew any
such stone, he is to be at liberty to do it,
if he first gives the owner of the land the

customary payment in consideration thereof.
(Monro's tr.)

xii. 1. 22. A loan of wine was made and
legal proceedings were taken to recover it.
. . . I asked to what locality the valuation
should refer. He [Sabinus] replied that if it
had been agreed that restoration should be
made at some particular place, the valuation
should follow the price at that place; if this
had not been settled, it should be according
to the place where the action was brought.
(Monro's tr.)

xiii. 3. 4. If the subject of the suit should
be goods of any kind which ought to have
been handed over on a given day, for example,
wine, oil or corn, then, according to Cassius,
the damages ought to be determined by the
value which they would have borne on the
day when the goods were to be handed over;
or, if no agreement was made as to the day,
then the value which they bore when issue
was joined; and a similar rule applies as to
place; so that an estimate should first be
made with reference to the place where the
goods were to be handed over, but, if there
was no agreement as to place, then the place
to be considered must be the one where the
action was brought. In fact this principle is
applied as to every kind of case. (Monro's tr.)

APPENDIX

xxi. 2. 6.   If an estate is sold, the security against defect in title should be given according to the custom of the place where the sale was made.

xxii. 1. 1.   When a judgment of good faith is reckoned up, the rate of interest is fixed by the decree of the judge according to the custom of the place where the contract was made; but so as not to offend the law.

(The place where the contract was made seems to mean, where the money was payable. — Gloss of Accursius.)

xxii. 5. 3.   In matters that have to do with calling witnesses, it is a requisite of diligence for the judge to find out the custom of the province in which he sits; for if it turns out that many persons are frequently summoned to give testimony from another city, there is no doubt that those should be summoned whom the judge deems necessary in the case.

xxv. 4. 1. § 15, end.   The custom of the place is to be regarded, and the womb should be inspected and the birth of the infant arranged by it.

xxvi. 1. 10.   A tutor out of the jurisdiction may be appointed, provided it is for a ward within the jurisdiction.

xxvi. 5. 1 *in fin*.   The president of a province

may give a tutor only to those who belong to his province or have a domicile there.

xxvi. 5. 27. In case of a ward who has property both at Rome and in a province, the praetor may appoint a tutor for the property in Rome, the president for that in the province.

xxvi. 7. 39. § 3. An heir appointed without a substitute died before he took up the inheritance, which he was to turn over to a child. The inheritance was in Italy, while the heir designate died in a province. I decided that the tutors of the provincial property should be convicted of negligence, if knowing the purpose of the will they abandoned the interests of the child; for if the trust in the inheritance had been carried out in the province, the purpose of the law would have been accomplished, and the administration of the property should have fallen to those who received the tutorship in Italy.

xxvi. 7. 47. Tutors for Italian property found, at Rome, instruments executed by provincial debtors, which provided that a sum of money should be paid at Rome, or wherever payment was demanded. I asked, where neither the debtors nor any property of theirs was in Italy, whether the collection of the debt belongs to the tutors for Italian property? I answered that if the contract were a provincial one the collection did not belong to them; but it was their duty to give information about the instruments to the tutors to whom the administration belonged.

xxviii. 1. 11. Hostages cannot make a will except by special permission.

xxix. 1 *ult.* The rescripts of the princes show that all who are of such a condition that they cannot make a will by military law, if they are seized and die in hostile territory may make a will as they will and can: whether it be the president of the province or anyone else who cannot make a will by military law.

xl. 1. 9. A slave cannot be manumitted who . . . has been made incapable of manumission by the prefect or a president for some delict.

xlii. 1. 15. § 1. The Emperor and his father have decided that the president of a province, if so ordered, shall execute a judgment given at Rome.

xlii. 5. 12. § 1. He who is adjudged to possess goods is so judged in that place of which the jurisdiction pertains to the judge.

xlviii. 22. 7. § 1. The presidents of provinces may banish to an island provided that the island is under their jurisdiction, that is, appertaining to their province; they may assign the island specially and banish to it.

But if they have none they shall sentence to banishment to an island, and write to the Emperor, that he may name the island. But they cannot banish to an island which they do not have within the province and under their authority.

xlviii. 22. 7. § 10. One may interdict from the province which he governs but not from another, and so the divine brothers [Verus and M. Antoninus] have said in a rescript. Whence it happened that one who was banished from the province where he was domiciled could dwell at his birthplace. But our Emperor with his divine father provided for this. For they wrote to Maecius Probus, president of the province of Spain, that one might be interdicted from the province of his birth by the ruler of the province in which he was domiciled. But this rescript applies in equity to nonresidents who commit offenses within a province.

xlviii. 22. 7. § 13. If one agrees with this opinion, that whoever commits a crime in a province may be banished by the ruler of that province, it will happen that a man so banished must keep away from three provinces as well as from Italy: namely, that in which he committed the offense, that in which he was domiciled, and his native province. And if he is found to have different native provinces, owing to his own condition and that of his father or relatives, we say that he is consequently banished from even more provinces.

l. 15. 4. § 2. He who has an estate in another city ought to declare [his property for taxation] in the city in which the property is; for he should pay the land tax to that city in whose territory his estate lies.

l. 16. 239. § 8. *Territory* is the entire amount of land within the boundaries of each city; which some say is so named because the magistrate of a place has the right of *terrifying*, that is, of exercising jurisdiction within those boundaries.

l. 17. 34. In stipulations and other contracts, that should always be done which was contracted; or if it is not clear what was intended, the custom of the place in which the contract was made should be followed. What then if the custom of the place is not clear, because usage varies? The obligation is then reduced to the least onerous interpretation.

EXTRACTS FROM THE CODE OF JUSTINIAN

1. 3. 10: If anyone commits sacrilege by breaking into churches or injuring priests and ministers, or does injury to the worship or the place, let his act be dealt with by the authorities of the province.

3. 15. 1. It is well known that prosecutions for crimes should be instituted where they were committed or initiated, or where the accused are found. (Auth. *qua in provincia*. In whatever province one commits a delict, or is guilty of money or of crimes, whether with respect to lands, or boundaries, possession, property, or mortgage, or any other matter, there let him be subject to the law.)

3. 24. 1. Whoever, being of high (though not illustrious) rank rapes a virgin or invades boundaries or is guilty of any other fault or crime, let him be dealt with by the public law within the province in which he perpetrated the deed, and make no use of his proper court; for guilt nullifies every honor of this sort.

5. 34. 2. It is clear law that a tutor born in another state and having no domicile where he is named cannot be sworn by one who has

no jurisdiction over him, whether by the president of another province or by municipal magistrates.

4. 42. 2. We forbid the transfer to the ownership of anyone in any way whatever of men of Roman race who have been made eunuchs, whether in barbarian or in Roman territory; and the most severe punishment is to be imposed upon those who have dared to do the act. . . . But we grant to all merchants or others the right to buy and sell in commerce, wherever they will, eunuchs of barbarian race, who have been made outside the territory subject to our jurisdiction.

8. 49 (48). 1. If the law of the city in which your father emancipated you gave such jurisdiction to the duumvirs that even foreigners might emancipate their sons, what your father did is binding.

8. 53 (52). Let the president of a province, hearing a suit, decide after proof of what has commonly been done in that very kind of suit in the town. For both a former custom and the reason which led to the custom are to be followed; and the president of the province will take care that nothing be done which is contrary to long continued custom.

9. 9. 15 Auth. But if because of the crime committed he hides or leaves the province

in which he offended, we command that he
be called by the judge with the lawful edicts,
and if he will not hear, that those proceedings
which are provided in our law be taken against
him. But if it is known that he is in another
province, we order that the judge of the province
in which the crime was committed use a
public letter to the judge of the province in
which he is. And he who receives the public
letter shall arrest him, at his own peril and of
his own office, and send him to the judge of the
province in which he offended, to be subjected
to the lawful punishment.

Novel. 17. 4. 2 and gloss:

[To the provincial officers]

If you find them [gl., the soldiers under your
charge] wrongdoers, besides every decent punishment
you will see that they make satisfaction
from their pay for all their wrongs [gl.,
committed in the province].

EXTRACTS FROM THE CANONS

Decretal 2. 2. 14:

You have asked the Apostolic See to explain whether priests having a church in one diocese and residing there but having a domicile by reason of property in another and there committing a wrong should be judged by him in whose diocese he has the property for the offense there committed; especially in cases which call for deprivation of his office or benefice? To this we answer shortly, that sentence must be given against him by the bishop in whose diocese he committed the offense; but execution is to be by him in whose diocese he holds a benefice.

Decretal 5. 39. 21 and gloss:

You ask us whether if one decrees as follows, whoever commits theft shall be excommunicated, this general clause refers to those under the jurisdiction of the excommunicator, or extends generally to all though not under his jurisdiction? We answer that this decree binds only those subject, unless perhaps where the greater and wider authority of the superior gives it such force.

Gloss. This seems wrong, because one comes under his jurisdiction by reason of the offense. . . . I answer that if this is to be understood generally, whoever commits theft anywhere, the clause refers only to subjects, as it says here; since one has no jurisdiction beyond his territory, and therefore the sentence does not extend beyond the bounds of his jurisdiction.

Sext. 1. 2. 2 gloss:

Suppose that my bishop makes a statute that no clerk should bear arms under pain of excommunication; a clerk who knew of the statute bore arms outside the diocese, and so acted against the statute; should he be subject to punishment? The Pontifex Romanus answered no; and said that statutes made by one who has limited territory do not have force outside the territory and the diocese, but only within the diocese.

EXTRACTS FROM THE SPECULUM JURIS

Book 2, Partic. 2, ver. 25 (ed. 1602, pt. ii, p. 662):

What about those [notaries] who are made by a bishop, a count, or a university? Note what my master [Azo] says in his Summa (ne clerici vel monach. § quae sunt sub § clericis etiam, ver. quid igitur *et seq.*) that a notary simply created by one who has the power of creation may use his office everywhere, just as a priest once ordained may celebrate everywhere once he is authorized by the license of the appointing power (ex. *de cleri. peregri.*); and voluntary jurisdiction is exercised everywhere. (Dig. *de off. procon. l.* 1 and 2; Dig. *de emancip. l. emancipati.*) But if it be argued as follows: I give you power to execute instruments within such a diocese, or province, the power cannot be exercised outside, just as an archbishop cannot use his *pallium* outside the province committed to him: my own opinion is, that even simple creation of an officer means creation within the territory of the creating officer.

[85]

BARTOLUS

Book 2, Partic. 3, § 5, ver. 2 (ed. 1602, pt. ii,
    p. 785):

Suppose a Fleming died at Genoa and there
in his will made his wife his heir. According
to the custom of Genoa a wife cannot succeed
her husband, and so the possessor of the goods
refuses to deliver them; but in Flanders there
is the contrary custom, and the woman takes.
Decide that the woman's case is best in ob-
taining the inheritance, according to the custom of Flanders, where she is bound.